W9-DDM-010

Understanding and Caring for Your Pet

Ferrets

MC

Understanding and Caring for Your Pet

Written by
Dr. Anne McBride BSc PhD Cert.Cons FRSA

Mason Crest
450 Parkway Drive, Suite D
Broomall, PA 19008
www.masoncrest.com
Developed and produced by Mason Crest

Printed and bound in the United States of America.

First printing
9 8 7 6 5 4 3 2 1

Series ISBN: 978-1-4222-3691-8
ISBN: 978-1-4222-3695-6
ebook ISBN: 978-1-4222-8087-4

Every reasonable care has been taken in the compilation of this publication.
The Publisher and Author cannot accept liability for any loss, damage, injury, or
death resulting from the keeping of ferrets by user(s) of this publication, or from
the use of any materials, equipment, methods, or information recommended in this
publication or from any errors or omissions that may be found in the text of this
publication or that may occur at a future date, except as expressly provided by law.
No animals were harmed in the making of this book.

Words in bold are explained in the glossary on page 127.

QR CODES AND LINKS TO THIRD PARTY CONTENT

You may gain access to certain third party content ("Third Party Sites") by scanning
and using the QR Codes that appear in this publication (the "QR Codes"). We do
not operate or control in any respect any information, products or services on such
Third Party Sites linked to by us via the QR Codes included in this publication, and
we assume no responsibility for any materials you may access using the QR Codes.
Your use of the QR Codes may be subject to terms, limitations, or restrictions set
forth in the applicable terms of use or otherwise established by the owners of the
Third Party Sites. Our linking to such Third Party Sites via the QR Codes does not
imply an endorsement or sponsorship of such Third Party Sites, or the information,
products or services offered on or through the Third Party Sites, nor does it imply
an endorsement or sponsorship of this publication by the owners of such Third
Party Sites.

Understanding and Caring for Your Pet

Educational Videos: Readers can view videos by scanning our QR codes, providing them with additional educational content to supplement the text. Examples include news coverage, moments in history, speeches, iconic moments, and much more!

Words to Understand: These words with their easy-to-understand definitions will increase the reader's understanding of the text, while building vocabulary skills.

Contents

Perfect Pets

Ferrets can be a lot of fun to keep as pets. They are lively, intelligent animals, although not particularly obedient. They come in a variety of colors and usually weigh between two and four pounds (900g–1.8kg).

After centuries of being kept as working animals, their popularity as pets has soared in recent times.

These are reasons why they can be attractive animals to keep:

- Ferrets are friendly animals that will enjoy being stroked if treated gently, and also enjoy playing with their owner.

- Ferrets live up to 10 years, and sometimes longer.

- Ferrets are not expensive to buy, and once you have bought your initial equipment, they are relatively inexpensive to feed and house, compared to a cat or dog.

Opposite:
Ferrets are inquisitive
and intelligent.

- However, you need to be aware that appropriate accommodation may not be cheap, and costs of feed and veterinary fees must be factored into your decision to keep ferrets. You may want to take out insurance to cover veterinary fees.

- Ferrets can be kept outside all year in temperate climates. The outside accommodation should comprise an enclosed hutch/cage area and a permanently attached run. The hutch must be kept warm and draft free, and must be sheltered from rain, the prevailing wind, and direct sunlight. Such outdoor ferret accommodation is often called a Ferret Court.

- Ferrets are frequently kept as house pets. They can live indoors, in a suitably sized cage with perma-nently attached exercise area. All ferrets must have the opportunity to exercise every day.

However, ferrets can be destructive and rather smelly, so they are not the right type of pet for everyone.

One word of warning. Ferrets can overheat easily and must be able to rest in cool places and have shade in the summer. They are most active around dawn and dusk, and may sleep for up to 20 hours a day, often very deeply.

Opposite:
If handled gently, ferrets can be friendly pets.

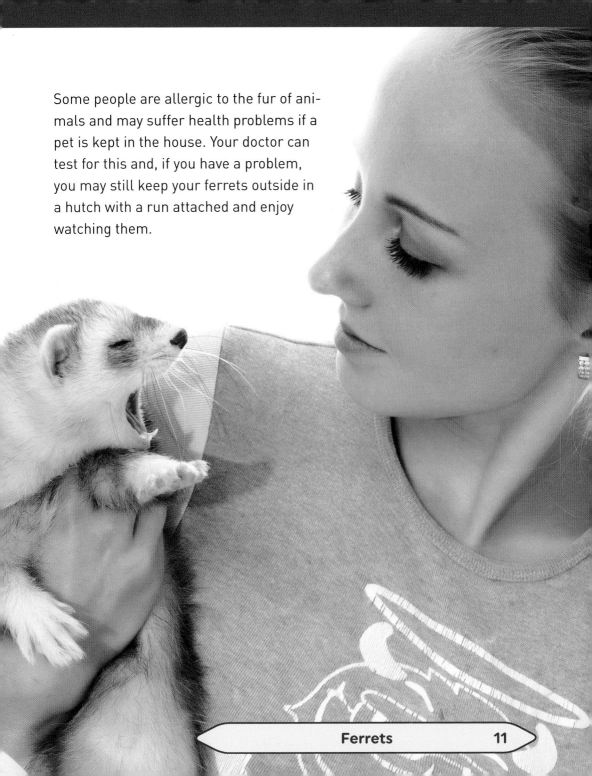

Some people are allergic to the fur of animals and may suffer health problems if a pet is kept in the house. Your doctor can test for this and, if you have a problem, you may still keep your ferrets outside in a hutch with a run attached and enjoy watching them.

Special Requirements

Ferrets are extremely appealing because of their mischievous characters and lively, playful behavior. But, like all animals, they have their own special requirements which you need to know about before buying your first ferrets.

This is important so you can have a good relationship with your ferrets, and they can live long, healthy and happy lives.

- You must handle your ferrets gently, even when playing with them. They are small animals and grabbing and squeezing will cause them pain. It could result in the ferret biting you or squirming out of your hand and being dropped, which is why they are not suitable pets for young children.

- You need to give your ferrets the right food to stay fit and healthy. Ferrets are true **carnivores** and cannot be fed a vegetarian diet.

- You will need to clean out the ferrets' home every day.

- You need to provide a large, safe area where your ferrets can exercise every day outside their hutch or cage.

- You will need to make arrangements for someone to look after your ferrets if you go away on vacation.

- You will need to register your ferrets with a veterinary practice. Ferrets need an annual vaccination against distemper, a disease that can kill, even if they are kept indoors. Every 18 months or so they will require hormone implants. **Neutering** ferrets is not recommended as they can develop a disease of the glands.

- You will need to check the ferret's coat, weight and nails every week.

- You will need to be able to commit to looking after your ferrets throughout their life, which may last ten years.

What is
a Ferret?

Wild ancestors

The wild ancestor of all our pet ferrets is the European polecat. Pet ferrets share the same basic behaviors and needs as their wild cousins. So in order to understand your ferrets, it is useful to know how their wild cousins live.

Polecats belong to the order Carnivora, the meat eaters, and the family Mustelidae. Interestingly, humans have only domesticated a few carnivore species as pets, namely dogs, (family Canis), cats (family Felis), and ferrets. The mustelid family is large and varied. It includes stoats, weasels, mink, otters and badgers.

A well-known mustelid is the endangered Giant Otter (Pteronura brasiliensis) from South America that can reach eight feet (2.4m) in length. Several mustelid species including the otter, stoat (ermine), and mink have been hunted by humans for their fur.

What is a ferret?

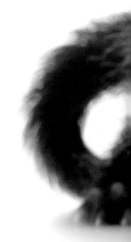

The fossil record shows that the European polecat (Mustela putorius) has been around for some 500,000 years, since the middle Pleistocene period, in western Europe. It is not often seen, as it is a solitary, nocturnal hunter. Like most mustelids, the polecat lives and hunts alone, though it shares its home range with other polecats and is far less territorial than other species. Its name "putorius" means smelly, from the Latin word for stench.

The polecat is short-legged and stocky, with a set of powerfully muscled jaws and strong, sharp teeth. Male and female polecats are sexually **dimorphic**—that is, they look different. In this case the difference is in size with males weighing up to four pounds (1.8kg) and females around one third lighter.

Polecats are obligate carnivores, which means their diet is based on the whole carcass of the animals they kill—meat, bones, guts, fur, and feathers. They are adept hunters. They stalk their prey and kill it with a bite to the neck. They hunt animals both above and below ground, and they eat a variety of items including birds, eggs, frogs, and rabbits. A polecat will even tackle animals much larger than itself, such as geese and hares. It also has a reputation for killing animals that are easy to catch such as chickens in a coop.

This latter habit earned it the French common name of *poulechat* (chicken cat), from which the name polecat is derived. In other countries, it was considered an enemy, and, until the invention of wire netting, a bounty was often paid for dead polecats.

Polecats are nocturnal hunters, and are most active at dusk and dawn. They share their hunting ground with other polecats, and have been recorded as traveling up to nine miles (14 km) in a single night. Throughout their area they have up to a dozen resting places—often under tree roots or shrubs, and in rabbit warrens. They rest here in the day away from the heat of the sun, or at night as a stop after they have eaten. They will also use such places to store food, and have been known to keep food items alive to eat later, particularly frogs and toads, by paralyzing them with a bite to the base of the skull.

Polecats have little in the way of social relationships other than males and females getting together to mate and the relationship between mother and her young, known as kits. Polecats are seasonal breeders, with the mating season occurring around the end of March.

Polecat courtship is minimal and mating is rather dramatic, though not romantic! The male will grab the female by the neck and pull her around. This is painful but stimulates ovulation. The male will mate with her, a process which can last for an hour. This process may happen several times until the female is pregnant. This is the end of the male's reproductive role and he will leave the female in search of another female.

Pregnancy lasts about 40 days after which a litter of five to 10 bald, blind, and deaf kittens will be born. The mother will stay with them for much of their early life and is very protective of them. When they are around three weeks old, the mother will start to bring prey items back for them to eat, and by eight weeks they have a full set of adult teeth and are fully weaned. When they are three months old they are fully independent and will set out to live on their own.

This page:
Ferrets are curious,
if a little cautious.

The Human Link

The ferret is the domesticated form of the polecat and its Latin name is _Mustela putorius furo_. As with most Latin names for animals, this reflects obvious characteristics of the species. Basically it means a smelly, thieving weasel!

Domestication has changed ferrets only slightly from their wild ancestors in terms of their behavior. Most notably, they are more social than polecats and can enjoy the company of other ferrets. They also remain playful into adulthood. They are less aggressive and less determined hunters than their polecat cousins.

Male ferrets are known as **hobs** and female ferrets are called **jills**.

Ferrets have been used for centuries for hunting rabbits and controlling rats. It has been suggested that they were first domesticated by the ancient Egyptians, but there is no evidence to support this, although no mummified ferrets have been found.

Opposite: Always ensure you carry your ferret safely.

The first historical records of ferrets are from the Greeks, and certainly the Romans used them for pest control.

Ferreting, that is hunting rabbits and other agricultural pests using ferrets, has been a popular pastime for many generations all over the world. Hunting was necessary in order to protect the crops when they are still growing from the unwanted attentions of rabbits. Ferrets also protected stored grain such as wheat and barley from mice and rats. Indeed, ferrets have been exported all around the world in attempts to control rabbit populations. However, hunting with ferrets is now illegal in the United States.

As far back as 1389, Gaston Phoebus wrote a beautifully illustrated book called the *Book of the Hunt* in which he describes how ferrets were used to hunt rabbits. The ferrets were muzzled and sent down the rabbit warren to drive the rabbits up to the surface and into nets.

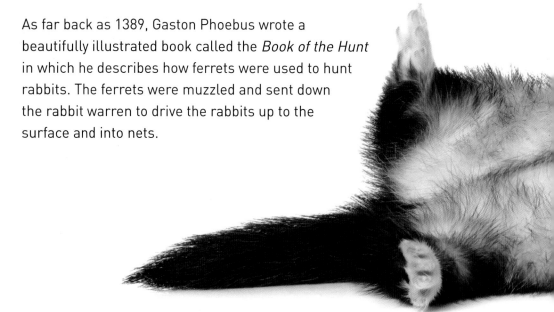

But this is not the only way humans have found ferrets to be useful. Ferrets share many features with humans, both anatomical and **physiological**, and can even catch influenza. They are used in medical research into a variety of conditions that can affect human health, including studies into influenza, swine flu, cystic fibrosis, and heart disease.

In the last 20 years, ferrets have become increasingly popular as pets and show animals. There are an estimated four million ferrets in the United States alone, though they are not legal to keep in every state. Overall, however, they are the most commonly kept mammal pet after dogs and cats.

The Ferret's World

This section describes how ferrets experience the world.

Nose

Ferrets are active during times of low light, so sight is not as important to ferrets as it is to animals that are out and about in daylight. Rather, the ferret lives in a world full of scent. It uses its acute sense of smell to find its way around its home, locate prey, and to identify other ferrets and animals, including humans, with which it lives.

When ferrets first meet, they will sniff and lick each other's hindquarters, as dogs do. They will also sniff each other's neck and ears. All of this sniffing lets them find out a lot about one another and enables them to recognize each other in the future. It is the ferret equivalent of humans shaking hands and introducing themselves.

Whiskers

The whiskers are used for touch, to measure the width of tunnels, nooks, and crannies, and to help the ferret find its way in the dark.

Head and mouth

The ferret head is long and fairly flat. This adds to the streamlined shape, which is ideal for running fast down tunnels after rabbits or rats. Also it means the jaws are large. The ferret's mouth can open wide, and its jaws are supported by strong muscles, which it uses in both biting and holding on to its prey or enemies if it is fighting, in pain, or scared.

Teeth

Ferrets have four types of teeth, evenly distributed on both sides. These are canines, incisors, premolars, and molars.

In the front are two pairs of canines. These are long and sharp and are used for killing prey, delivering the deadly neck bite.

Between the canines, right at the front of the mouth, is a row of very small, pointed incisors, six on the top jaw and six on the bottom. These are used for grooming.

Behind the canines are the 12 pre-molars, three on each side, top and bottom. These work with a scissor action and are used to slice meat and chop it into bite size pieces.

Finally, in the back of the mouth are the molars. There are six of these, one on each side of the top jaw and two on each side of the bottom. These are large and flatter shaped and are used for crushing and grinding food.

The teeth of ferrets do not grow continuously, as they do in many rodents.

Eyes

The ferret's eyes are well adapted to its lifestyle. They are located in the front, but slightly to the side and top of the head. This means not only do ferrets see well in front of them, but also have almost all-around vision, so they can be on the lookout for prey, and enemies, on all sides. Ferrets do not have good color vision, but do have good depth perception because their eyes point forward.

As animals that are active in semi-dark conditions, they are sensitive to bright lights. The eyes are also very sensitive to movement, and particularly movement that may mean dinner! The pupil is slit shaped, like a cat's, but is also at an angle in the eye. The angle of the pupil means it will respond to movement of animals that move both horizontally and vertically, such as in hopping motions. This is the typical movement of the prey of ferrets, such as mice, frogs, and rabbits.

This may explain why ferrets sometimes have the reputation for being rather quick to nip fingers. Basically, their sight for recognizing objects is not good and their instinctive reaction to something that moves fast in their field of vision is to grab it with their teeth.

Ears

Ferrets hear sounds at a higher pitch than we do. They can hear things we cannot, such as the ultrasonic squeaks of mice, but may not pick up the sound of a deep voice. Their sense of hearing is extremely well developed, and they use it to detect prey and also to create a sound map of their environment.

Legs

A ferret's body is long and slim, with legs that almost seem too short for it. However, these legs are powerful and, along with a supple and strong back, enable them to be very agile creatures, though they are not very good climbers. The short legs mean that a ferret can carry prey items which may be two or three times bigger than it, without tripping over the load.

Feet

Ferrets use their front feet for climbing and for holding onto objects. They have long nails on their feet, which they would normally wear down as they move around or dig in the earth.

Movement

Ferrets are extremely agile creatures and are able to turn around in extremely small places. They can jump and twist in the air and can arch their backs in a manner that resembles drawings of a witch's cat.

Tail

The ferret's tail is not particularly long and is used primarily for balance. It also uses its tail to communicate how it is feeling.

Body

The long, slim body of the ferret means that it can get into very small spaces. The back and neck muscles are very strong enabling it to be fast and agile, and to carry large items of prey.

Odor

Ferrets, especially unneutered males, are renowned for being smelly creatures. They have a distinctive musty odor. This is due to the scent emitted from skin glands distributed all over the body, which in the males also makes the coat feel sticky. This is particularly noticeable in the breeding season, and is one reason why people have male ferrets neutered. Neutering can reduce this smell, but it will not get rid of it entirely.

Ferrets also have anal glands, which they can empty very quickly when they are frightened. The strong smell is meant to deter an enemy. In some countries, veterinarians surgically remove these glands.

Coat

The ferret's coat is thick, with an insulating undercoat, covered with guard hairs. It is well designed to keep ferrets warm at night when they are out and about. Recently, people have begun breeding ferrets with a short Rex coat, or a long Angora coat. Both of these types are rare as they are mutations and only maintained through inbreeding. They require extra care, and are not suitable for life outdoors.

Opposite:
Come on, let's play!

Colors and Markings

Ferrets have been bred to come in five main colors, though some show groups will recognize variations on these themes as distinct colors.

Polecat or fitch

This coloration resembles that of the wild polecat. (In Great Britain, this is known as Fitch to avoid any misunderstanding when talking about the wild species or a colored ferret.) The legs of a polecat-colored ferret are dark and it will have a dark mask across its eyes, known as the robber's mask. This coloring is a perfect camouflage for a nighttime predator.

Albino or English ferret

These white ferrets are a favorite of people who work their ferrets for hunting, as they are easier to see in the dark.

Top:
Polecat or Fitch

Bottom:
Albino

True albinos have red eyes. In unneutered albinos, the coat is often an apricot or orangey color.

Albinism can be associated with poor sight and/or poor hearing.

Dew or dark-eyed white

Like the Albino, the coat is pure white. However, the eyes are black or a dark ruby-red, making a dramatic contrast.

Silver or grey

This is a less common color variation. Often these ferrets will have white markings on the chest or feet. The eyes are dark ruby-red. Variations on this basic silver color include silver-mink, silver-bib and silver-mitt.

Sandy

This encompasses a range of coat color tone from a light brown to a deep golden color. Sandy colored ferrets may have darker limbs and a mask like a polecat. Variations of the sandy color include cinnamon, copper, and champagne.

Opposite:
Silver or Grey (Top)

Dark-Eyed White (Middle)

Sandy (Bottom)

One Ferret or Two?

The need to provide our ferrets with suitable company is part of our responsibility for caring for them. In the case of ferrets, that suitable company may be yours.

F errets are more social than their polecat cousins, but they can be kept happily as solitary pets, so long as you ensure you give them sufficient time with you every day. Indeed, the ferret's natural state would be as a solitary animal that only really interacts with other ferrets to reproduce.

Ferrets that have been kept with other ferrets since they were young can be kept in pairs or groups. When keeping animals in groups of males and females, it is important to ensure that unwanted babies are not born. With other animals, such as dogs, neutering is the normal way of dealing with this.

However, with ferrets it is not as simple. Indeed, whether you keep one or several, understanding their reproductive biology is important to keep them healthy.

Neutering

Ferret reproductive biology is quite complex and recent research has shown that neutering both males and females may affect their long-term health by making them more likely to develop tumors when they mature. The breeding season in ferrets is triggered by daylight length and, while neutering removes the testes and ovaries, it does not stop other hormones in the body being produced as the days lengthen. These would normally trigger activity in the ovaries and testes, but as these are no longer there in the neutered animal, the adrenal glands become overstimulated.

Ideally, they should not be neutered and certainly not before they reach puberty, as the earlier they are neutered the sooner they will develop adrenal disease. Adrenal tumours are very difficult to treat, usually requiring an operation, or long term medication. If not detected early enough they can be fatal.

In natural circumstances, the jill will come into season around March, and will stay in season until she is mated, or until the daylight length takes her out of season several months later. When in season the jill produces high levels of a hormone called estrogen. If the female is not successfully mated then she will continue to produce estrogen, and this can cause her to die from estrogen-associated anemia.

Thanks to recent veterinary developments, there is now a solution, known as the "jill-jab," which brings the female out of season. This injection is given when the female comes into season and ends the season in a week or two. Usually, only one jill-jab is needed each year, though some years, where there is a particularly warm and sunny autumn for example, the female may come back into season and need a further injection.

An alternative is an implant which is inserted just below the ferret's skin. This releases a hormone slowly over 18–24 months which stops the jill coming into season, but the owner must look out for signs of season at the end of this time.

This implant can also be used with male ferrets as a form of chemical **castration**. As with surgical castration, this will help reduce the male ferret smell, and help avoid adrenal gland disease.

If a ferret of either gender has been surgically neutered, then the implant regime is important to help delay the onset of adrenal disease.

Vasectomy is another way in which males and entire female ferrets can be kept together without offspring. However, this does not reduce the smell of the male and is not the usual choice of those wanting pet ferrets. This is because the male will still mate with the female.

To summarize, if you want to keep one or more ferrets then:

—Females will need to have a jill-jab yearly or an implant. They can be kept either as a single animal or in groups. They are not as odorous as males and thus more suitable as house pets, though they are not entirely scent free!

—Males should be not be "fixed," and therefore are more suitable kept outdoors, as they will be rather smelly. Males who have known each other from young can be kept together.

If you want to keep males and females together, both sexes should have the implant.

Ferrets and other pets

Ferrets can live with dogs and cats, though neither may particularly appreciate the ferret's insistence on playing ferret games! Cats will tend to remove themselves when they have had enough, but dogs may show their frustration and bite back. Ferrets and dogs or cats should always be supervised when together to avoid the potential for fighting and injury.

Ferrets cannot be kept with small mammals, or birds. After all, they are predators and are highly likely to kill pets such as rabbits, guinea pigs, hamsters, finches, parakeets, or even parrots given the slightest opportunity.

Setting Up Home

Before you buy your ferrets, you will need to decide where you are going to keep them, and then buy suitable housing. Ferrets tolerate cooler conditions better than hot ones, and the ideal temperature range is 50–68°F (10–20°C). They can cope with colder conditions, even snow, if their home is not damp or drafty and they have plenty of bedding.

Setting up a good home for your ferret.

Remember, too, that ferrets easily suffer from heat-stroke. Accommodation should be well ventilated, but not drafty, and be in the shade.

Whether you keep your ferrets inside or out, the accommodation must have both a safe sleeping area (a hutch or cage) and a permanently attached exercise area (run) that they can get to when they wish.

You may also have safe areas where they can go free in your home. There are commercially available wooden hutch/run combinations available for ferrets, as there are for rabbits. Indeed, those designed for rabbits are also suitable for ferrets.

The Great Outdoors

Ferrets can live in an outside hutch-and-run complex all year round, as long as temperatures do not get too extreme. These ferret enclosures, or courts, must provide shelter from the prevailing wind and direct sunshine. Ferrets need somewhere cool and shady in hot weather so their home should not be in direct sunlight. On hot, sunny days, a reflective cover should be put over the sleeping quarters to help keep the ferrets cool.

- The enclosure must be made secure to prevent your ferrets escaping. Ferrets can wriggle through a very small hole and, if wire mesh is used on either the hutch or the run, the holes must be small enough to prevent the ferret pushing its head through. As ferrets are not prone to chewing, the mesh does not have to be wide gauge. Likewise, ferrets are not great diggers, so the floor of the exercise part of their court does not have to be underwired, but the wire walls do need to be buried several inches.

- The sleeping area (hutch) should be raised off the ground to prevent dampness and drafts.

- It should be lined with newspaper, sawdust, or wood shavings to help keep it dry and draft-free. Do not use sand as a lining, as it may stick to some of your ferret's food and cause gut problems if swallowed.

- Your ferret's bedding should go on top of the lining. This can be hay or straw, or shredded paper. Even shredded newspaper is fine, though the ink may rub off on to the fur, giving lighter colored ferrets a greyish hue. Bedding should be dust free to avoid any respiratory illness developing.

Opposite:
A favorite and safe
look-out spot.

- Other bedding materials available are towels or Vetbed, but these must be checked for loose fibers which your ferret may accidentally swallow, again leading to gut problems.

- Hammocks suspended in the sleeping area are a firm favorite with ferrets.

- A water bottle for small animals should be fitted to the side of the hutch. Fresh water must always be available for your ferret. Water bowls are not always suitable as they can be spilled or filled with bedding.

- However, ferrets do enjoy drinking from bowls, playing and bathing in water, as well as tipping over water bowls! If you want to provide your ferret with a water bowl, do so in its run, not its sleeping area. Use a heavy type, and you may find putting in a large stone helps keep it upright! Do not place it near your ferret's chosen toilet area.

In the winter use a hutch cover to reduce heat escaping from the roof. This will provide extra protection from the cold. The cover can be pulled down to cover the front of the hutch at night, still allowing sufficient fresh air. In cold weather, make sure the ferret's water has not frozen—wrapping the bottle will help protect it from freezing. Ensure the sipper is not frozen and the water can flow. You may wish to provide an insulated bowl of water too. Your ferret needs to be able to have fresh drinking water at all times.

In the summer, make sure they have plenty of water. If it gets really hot, wrap a towel around a plastic bottle filled with iced water, and place it in their sleeping area so they can lie next to it to stay cool. Providing tiling slabs for your ferrets to lie on will also help keep them cool.

Outside run

Ideally a run should be permanently attached to the hutch so your ferrets have free access to it and can choose to go out at will. They should be given the opportunity to exercise for several hours a day, in the evening or very early morning.

The run should be as big as possible, with a covered area at one end. If the run is separate from the hutch, remember to attach a water bottle to the side of it.

If the run is on grass, make sure the surface has not been treated with pesticides.

If it is on concrete, provide an area filled with children's play sand or soil so your ferret has a soft resting place.

The run should also contain items for your ferrets to use and play with. Logs to sit on will enable them to see further and detect scents on the breeze.

Opposite:
Ferrets love to explore.

Half pipes and tunnel systems will help keep them busy, especially if you sometimes rearrange the layout. These should have drainage holes to stop them becoming flooded. You can buy tunnel systems or make your own using PVC tubing, U-bends, and T-junctions. Ferrets are climbers, and will enjoy using all the space provided. Gently sloping ramps can be incorporated into the run. Toys are also important, and, like other predator pets, ferrets like toys that move. Ping-pong balls, paper bags, and toys for small dogs are all appropriate, but make sure they are not made of latex or foam rubber because these may be chewed and small pieces swallowed.

Litter trays

Ferrets are naturally clean animals and they tend to use the same places for their toilet. They are not able to be house trained in the same way a dog or cat, but they can be taught where to go and litter trays can be used as latrines. Ferrets naturally have several latrine sites, and these tend to be chosen in corners of their enclosure. Because ferrets normally defecate by lifting their tails and squirting feces upwards, ferret litter trays are normally triangular in shape with two high sides. They can thus be fitted neatly in the corners chosen by your ferret.

The floor of the litter tray can be covered with paper, sawdust, wood shavings, soil, or a sand/soil mix or a non-scented, dust-free commercial cat litter. It is important not to use scented cat litter, as this can have a chemical reaction with the ferret's deposits, causing discomfort to your pet.

House Ferrets

Many owners like to keep their ferrets indoors, but their requirements for a secure, dark, ventilated sleeping area, a place to exercise freely, latrine sites, and plenty of things to do are the same.

If you are thinking of keeping your ferrets indoors, be prepared for the ferret smell. This can be reduced by cleaning all the bedding every few days, and litter trays every day. Shredded paper bedding is usually easier to cope with than hay or straw. In addition, to help control the smell, the litter trays will need to be cleaned every time they are used. Do not try and solve the problem with air fresheners, as these can cause respiratory problems for your pet.

Hutches and adjoining runs can also be used indoors. Though they will not need to be weather-proofed from the cold, it is important that your ferret's home does not

get too hot. It should not be in direct sunlight nor close to radiators or fires. Remember that if your ferrets only have a small area to live in, they must be given the opportunity to exercise for several hours a day.

Ferret-proofing your home

Whether your ferret has free access to a room in your home all the time, or you simply let it out of its hutch for exercise and play, the room must be ferret proofed.

If you let your ferrets go free indoors, cover up trailing electric wires, and put away any objects that may be chewed and harmful bits swallowed. Ferrets should always be closely supervised when out and about, and remember there will need to be litter trays in every room.

Taking Your
Ferret Out
and About

Microchipping

Ferrets are great escape artists, so it is strongly advised that you have your ferret **microchipped**. Also, if your ferret has distinctive markings, make sure you have a clear photograph to aid identification.

Ferrets can wear specially designed collars to which you attach a tag. But collars can come off, and name tags can be lost or chewed by the ferret, so microchipping is best.

Harness and lead

Ferrets are not dogs. If you want to take them out for a walk off-leash, there is a good chance that you will lose your pets as they scoot away to explore and, most probably, disappear down a hole. They are independent characters and are not likely to come back to you when you call just because you think it is time to go home.

It is sensible to train your ferret to wear a harness and lead. These should be used every time you take your pet somewhere that is not ferret-proofed. There are many ferret harnesses to choose from. Ask for advice about correct fitting. Avoid jerking the lead when you walk your ferret or you may damage his neck.

Opposite:
Teach your ferret to walk in a harness on a loose lead.

Ferret fun

You may simply want to take your ferret out with you for a walk. Alternatively, you may wish to show or race your pet. There are many ferret associations that run shows, judging individual ferrets on their color and general **conformation**. They also hold fun events such as ferret races. These are often held at country fairs to help raise money for ferret rescue charities or for research into ferret care. The the American Ferret Association will be able to help you find a local group.

Finding Your Ferrets

Ferrets might be available at your local pet store. They will be kept in spacious runs so you will have the opportunity to watch them and make your choice.

You could consider giving an unwanted ferret a new home. Many pet stores now have adoption centers and, of course, there are many associations that are constantly looking to find homes for unwanted pets.

If you want a particular color which is not available at your pet store, you could try a local ferret rescue group, or contact the American Ferret Association to find your nearest reputable breeder.

Opposite:
A group of ferrets is
called a "business"!

Signs of a healthy ferret

Check that the ferrets you choose are fit and well.

Mouth

There should be no signs of broken teeth, which could mean the ferret will develop dental problems.

Eyes

Look for bright, clear eyes, with no discharge.

Ears

Check the inside of the ears to see if they look and smell clean. There should be no sign of damage on the outer ear.

Nose

The nose should be cold and a little moist, similar to a dog's nose.

Coat

The coat should be clean and glossy, with no scurf or bald patches. It should feel soft to touch. The skin beneath should be a light pink color.

Body

The body should be well covered, with no lumps or swellings. The ferret should naturally look slim and almost tube-like in shape.

Tail

Check under the tail for any matting or soiling, which could indicate diarrhea (see Health section).

Breathing

Watch the ferret's breathing. A healthy ferret takes between 30 and 40 breaths a minute, and breathing should be quiet and regular.

Movement

The ferret has an ambling gait when walking, and there should be no sign of lameness.

Taking Your Ferret Home

It is important that your ferret's new home is set up and ready for him beforehand. When you first bring your ferret home, you will want to stroke and play with him, but you must be patient. For the first few days, your ferret will need peace and quiet to get used to his new home.

You will need to provide food, and change the water, so your ferret will start getting used to you without the stress of being handled. You could whistle gently or call his name before you put the food down. He will soon learn to come when called, as he associates your whistle with something pleasant.

Ferrets do not enjoy being picked up from their cage, and may tell you so with a nip or two. It is far better to let them come partially out of the cage toward you and then pick them up.

If you spend time getting to know your ferrets, they will become more relaxed and will like to interact with you. When your ferrets appear to be happy and relaxed, you can start making friends.

- To begin with, come close to the hutch or cage, and talk to your ferret. Do not make any sudden movements which will alarm him.

- Offer treats, so the ferret has to come up to you, and gets used to your hand.

- Let the ferret come all the way to you, and then pick him up.

Ferrets that are handled properly and from an early age can be very affectionate creatures, though not all will appreciate being cuddled. They can however, enjoy being carried around.

Ferrets need to be carried in such a way that their body weight is supported. Place one hand underneath the chest, with a finger either side of his front legs, and the other around his hindquarters, or along his belly. Using the hand underneath his chest, lift upwards and use your other hand to support his weight.

Be careful when passing a ferret from one person to another while you are standing, as the height and motion can be frightening and cause him to panic. A frightened ferret can move very fast, may bite and potentially be dropped or squeezed too hard as you try to stop him escaping. Squeezing can cause damage to the internal organs, or break ribs.

Playtime

Whether ferrets are kept in the house or outside, they should be given the chance to behave naturally. Ferrets are extremely inquisitive and active creatures and need to have room to move and things to do.

77

O nce you have made friends there are many things that you and your ferrets can do together. You may even wish to teach them tricks. This can be a great way of bonding with your ferrets, and is lots of fun.

Ferrets can be taught to come when called, go to bed, roll over, sit up on their hind legs, do an obstacle course (ferret agility), and even fetch a ball or other toy. It is also a useful way of teaching your ferret to be relaxed for health checks.

Clicker training

Just like dogs, ferrets respond well to clicker training, a reward-based system originally developed in America by Karen Pryor when she was working with dolphins.

Karen wanted to mark "correct" behavior at the moment it happened. She found it was impossible to toss a fish to a dolphin when it was in midair, when she wanted to reward it. Her aim was to establish a conditioned response so the dolphin knew it had performed correctly and a reward would follow.

Clicker training basics.

The solution was the clicker—a small, matchbox-shaped training aid with a metal tongue that makes a click when it is pressed. To begin with, the dolphin had to learn that click meant that food was coming. The dolphin then learned that it must earn a click to get a reward.

Clicker training has been used with many different animals and it has proved hugely successful. The intelligent ferret takes to it well. You'll need a clicker and treats.

For further information check out, **www.clickertraining.com**

Ferret fun

You can help your ferrets to live a full life by doing the following:

- Give your ferrets plenty of new things to do. Ferrets are such intelligent creatures that they get bored easily. If you do not provide them with appropriate entertainment, they are sure to find mischief, and it is unlikely that you will appreciate it!

- Make a dig box—a cardboard box filled with scrunched up paper, hay, or straw, with some holes cut in the sides. Your ferret will enjoy squirming in and out of the box. You can even scatter some dry ferret food for it to find among the paper.

- A pillowcase with cellophane inside will provide a lot of fun as the ferret dances over it, stimulated by the crackling sound of the cellophane.

- Make a ferret "apple bobbing" game. This is simply a large bowl or tub with about 4 inches (10 cm) of water in the bottom and some ping-pong balls in it. Make sure the ferrets can get in and out easily, then sit back and watch the fun.

Make a slide using a gently-sloping piece of PVC tubing, from sofa height to the floor. Your ferret will enjoy whizzing down this.

Ferret Behavior

One of the most rewarding things about owning a pet is learning to understand what it is thinking or feeling. This will also help you detect if your ferret is not feeling well.

If you have two or more ferrets, you will witness natural behavior as they interact with each other. But you can also learn a lot about a single ferret by watching how he moves, the postures he adopts, and listening to the sounds he makes. Ferrets are not noisy, and communicate more through their body language.

Relaxed and happy ferrets

A happy and relaxed ferret is a joy to have around. He will be curious about his world and wander about with his head up, taking in all the sights, sounds, and smells. He may wag his tail as he investigates some new object or opening. Your ferret will often make quiet little chuckling or clucking sounds as he explores. Ferrets use their mouths like we use our hands to investigate new objects. This is one of the reasons why they are considered so destructive—everything has to be nibbled!

He will scent mark the ground and objects by pushing his body along with his hind legs. His face will run along the surface as he leaves a trail of scent from the glands under the chin. It looks like he is pretending to plow the ground!

When he decides to rest, the relaxed ferret will close his eyes, stretch out his front legs and spread out his toes—a perfect picture of peace and contentment.

When ferrets wake up they often seem to shiver. Actually this rapid shaking is normal and not to be confused with your pet suffering a fit. Ferrets will also show this shaking when they are excited or frightened.

A bottle brush tail, or hair raised along the neck and back, can have two meanings. Either your ferret is excited or pleased, (for example, enjoying being gently scratched) or it is a sign of fear.

Ferrets are very active when they are awake. You may find your ferret doing all sorts of things to get your attention, such as rattling his water bottle (check that it is not empty), nibbling your fingers or inviting you or another ferret to play.

An invitation to play is not subtle, and basically consists of jumping on the potential playmate! Another invitation is delivered in the form of the so-called "war dance of the weasel." This can also be an expression of joy with the world and a way of letting off steam.

One ferret will stand upright in front of the other (or you), opening his mouth wide without baring his teeth, and then jump vertically off the ground, or bounce from his front to his back feet repeatedly. All the time he twists his body as he jumps and shakes his head vigorously. He looks as though he has gone completely crazy as he falls and knocks into objects. If the other ferret takes up the invitation, then a rough-and-tumble play fight will start with both ferrets rolling around on the floor and play biting each other. An alternative game is that of tag, or chase. Ferrets who want to play can be very insistent!

Angry ferrets

A ferret that does not want to play or interact will turn away, perhaps hiss or open his mouth, drawing his lips back to show his teeth.

A ferret that simply has had enough attention from another, or from you, will prod with his nose. He may arch his back and push sideways up against the other, as a half-hearted challenge to fight about the point.

The ferret who is moving very slowly, low to the ground, is trying not to be noticed. He just wants to be left alone.

Frightened ferrets

A ferret that is frightened may show a bottle brush tail in an attempt to look bigger. Ferrets will attack when they are threatened by something that scares them. He may lie flat on the floor, ready to spring, making a yapping sound. This is a warning that he may bite, so watch out!

A ferret with its back arched and tail upright, like a cat, is saying that he is frightened and prepared to defend himself. He will make a screaming sound as a further warning, and if that does not cause the threat to go away then be prepared for an attack.

Food,
Glorious Food

A well-balanced diet will keep your ferrets healthy, and will help to ensure a good, long life. It is very important not to overfeed, particularly if you have house ferrets. Ferrets living outside need more food to give them the energy to stay warm. House ferrets do not need to do this, and will easily become overweight and obese (see Health).

Naturally, ferrets eat animals that they have killed. They are obligate carnivores and in order to get a balanced diet, they eat the whole animal, not just the meat. Being an obligate carnivore, like cats, means they cannot live on dog food or a vegetarian diet. Nor is processed meat such as bacon, sausages, and salami suitable for ferrets. Indeed, most human foods will do harm to your ferrets and should not be given even as treats.

While it is possible to feed your ferret a natural diet of fresh/frozen **carcasses** of rodents and day-old chicks, or freshly-killed wild rabbit, it is not what everyone wants to do. Frozen carcasses are available from pet stores. The advantage is that it is a natural food which will occupy the ferret's time as well as filling its belly.

The two main disadvantages are that frozen rodents are very high in fat, and the mess/hygiene issues that will be created. The carcass cannot be allowed to go bad while it is defrosting and any uneaten food left in the bowl or stashed away by the ferret must be removed quickly, especially in warm weather, as it will attract flies and disease.

A vet shows how to feed a ferret.

There are however, several dry diets available. You should check the packet ingredients to ensure it states that the protein is animal-derived and that it meets the dietary needs of ferrets. They require a diet that contains about 40% animal-based protein, more than 20% fat, and less than 25% carbohydrate. They need only a small amount of fiber, making up about 10-15% of the diet. Essential micronutrients include amino acids, especially taurine, calcium and phosphorous.

If you find uneaten food that your ferret has stashed away, then you are feeding him too much. Your weekly weight check should also indicate if you are feeding the right amount. If your ferret is gaining weight, your obesity alarm should be alerted.

Dry food does have its own drawbacks. It has a shelf life—a use by date. Food used after this may have lost its nutritional value and no longer be a healthy diet for your ferret. As it is a dry food, your ferret will drink more. Finally, from a ferret's viewpoint, dry food in a bowl is rather boring. It can be made more interesting by filling small dog activity balls with the daily ration. Your pet will learn to roll the ball along to release the treats. Alternatively, scatter the dry food around the ferret's home so he can use his nose to find it in a highly rewarding game.

Treats

Only give your ferret healthy treats. These can be raw bones, or a raw egg in its shell. Raw eggs are a natural food and will occupy your ferret for quite some time as he rolls it around and bites it carefully so he can finally enjoy the contents.

If you are going to teach your ferret tricks, training treats can be small pieces of plain boiled or roast chicken. You can buy ready-made ferret treats, but make sure they are almost entirely made from meat.

Ferret Care

Looking after ferrets means keeping their house clean and keeping a close watch for health problems. Ferrets can live for up to 15 years, but sadly many only live for about half that time. This may be because owners do not understand the needs of ferrets and may not provide a suitable diet and or the right place for them to live.

Handling your pet every day and performing regular health checks will help you pick up on the early signs of ill health and enable you to take action quickly to treat ailments before they become too serious. This is best done while handling your pet in the normal way. You should do any examinations as part of your grooming and regular play.

Weigh your ferrets on a regular basis and keep a record of their weight. Once they are fully grown, females should have a reasonably stable weight. Males however, tend to increase their weight quite dramatically at the start of the breeding season in late spring. Put your ferret in a small, securely-closed box on the scales and note the weight. Then weigh the box without the ferret. The difference between the two is your ferret's weight.

You should know how your pet behaves while healthy. Changes from normal behavior can also indicate ill health. These may include being less active, being unsteady when walking, showing changes in eating or drinking habits, hiding more, or becoming aggressive.

Though ferrets are predators, they are solitary hunters and thus have to hunt and feed themselves even when in pain. They are good at disguising signs of illness, so familiarity with your own pets is vital. As a guide, signs of illness in a ferret include:

- A dull, dry, matted coat.
- Bald patches of missing fur.
- Red, moist or flaky skin.
- Scratching more than usual.
- Disinterest in food.

- Drinking less than usual.
- Drinking more than usual.
- Less playful, inquisitive, or active than normal.
- Eyes are dull not bright and shining.
- Wheezing.
- Dribbling mouth.
- Pawing at his mouth.
- Change in the consistency of feces.
- Red colored urine.
- Vomiting.
- Fits.
- A runny nose, watery eyes, coughing, and sneezing.
- Swollen, painful stomach area.
- Swollen genitals in females.

You should seek veterinary help sooner rather than later. It may mean the difference between a speedy recovery for your ferret, or possibly a long (and expensive) treatment. Some conditions if not treated early, may mean your ferret will not survive.

Whether you are going to the vet for a check up, vaccination or because your ferret is ill, take him in a secure box designed for ferrets or a cat carrying box.

Daily tasks

- Remove all uneaten food, and wash the feed bowls. If you frequently find uneaten food in the bowls, or more likely stashed away around the hutch, it may mean you are feeding too much. Give less next time. But do check that your ferret is eating and is not unwell.

- Refill the water bottle with fresh water. Check that your ferret is drinking from the bottle, if not it may be that he is unwell. It is worth noting how much you usually have to put in the bottle so that you will notice if your ferret is drinking more or less than normal.

- Remove soiled litter from the litter tray, wash the tray and put in clean litter. Do not use strong-smelling cleaning fluids as this may put your ferret off using the tray. Check the feces are normal and any urine is not red in color (see Health section).

Give your ferret(s) access to the exercise area for several hours a day. Spend some time watching and interacting with them. If your ferret is less active than normal it may not be well.

Opposite:
Beware: ferrets are
great escape artists.

Weekly tasks

- Confine your ferrets to the exercise area so you can clean the cage or hutch thoroughly.

- Remove all bedding and clean out the cage or hutch with an animal-friendly disinfectant. Clean the water bottle and then refill it.

- Replace all bedding material.

- Check your ferret's nails and clip them if they are too long.

- Groom your ferrets. Check for ticks, fleas, and any sore or bald patches.

- Weigh your ferret to check whether it is losing or gaining weight.

Nosy is the ferret's middle name!

Grooming

The amount of grooming each ferret needs depends on the season, coat density, and length. If you have an Angora, it will require more attention than a normal coated ferret.

All ferrets benefit from a weekly brushing, especially when they are molting. Grooming helps keep the coat and underlying skin healthy. It also helps prevent your ferret swallowing too much fur and developing hairballs that can block his guts and require surgery. It also enables you to check for any problems, and, if you do it properly, this should be an enjoyable experience for you and your ferret.

A cat-grooming brush is ideal for a ferret. Be careful not to press too hard when you groom your ferret, or you may hurt him. He will soon tell you if you are using too much pressure . . . often with a quick nip!

Grooming tips for comfort and safety.

Ears

It is normal for ferrets to produce a lot of ear wax. This can be gently cleaned from the outer ear using a cotton swab with a few drops of baby oil on it. DO NOT put the baby oil directly into your ferret's ear and DO NOT try and stick the cotton swab down the ferret's ear. You may do serious damage, cause your pet a lot of pain and be bitten in the process. Only clean the part of the ear that you can see.

Nails

Naturally, a ferret would keep its nails in trim by running over the ground and through the underground tunnels of a rabbit warren. A pet ferret's nails may grow too long, which will make moving very uncomfortable as they can curve over and dig into the feet or distort the ferret's toes. Placing some rougher surfaces in your ferret's exercise area can help keep nails in good condition. A simple way is to put a few concrete paving stones to walk on or a series of brick platforms they can climb over. Putting their food on this means they will have to get on to and walk on the rough surface, which will help wear their nails.

Opposite:
Check and clean
the outer ear.

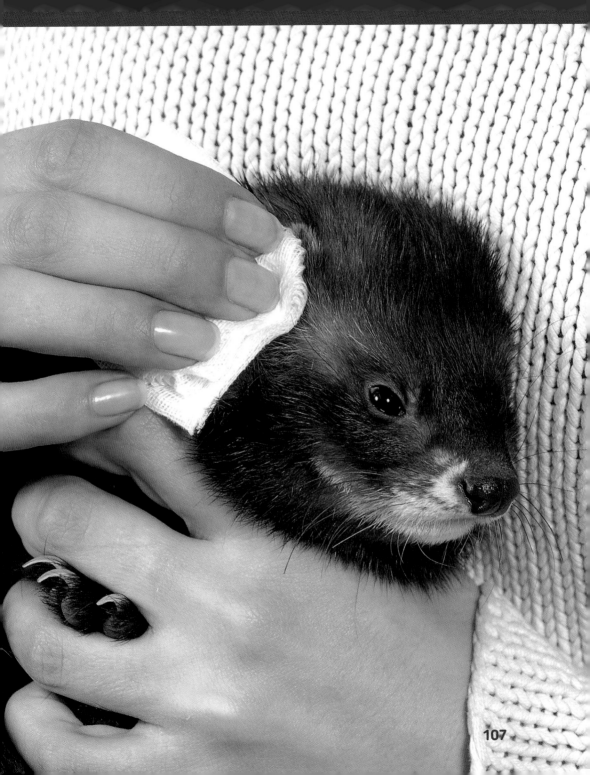

Nails can be clipped with special clippers, similar to those used for dogs, but you will need to ask a vet or an experienced ferret-keeper to do this for you, or show you how to do it. You must be careful not to cut an adjacent toe or cut the nail too short to the **quick** or nail-bed. This is pink colored as it contains blood vessels, and nerves. While easy to see on light colored nails, on dark nails it can be difficult to judge where the quick is. In that case, trim the nails to the same length as any white ones or just remove the tip. The small size of ferrets makes this quite a difficult job.

Cutting the nail-bed by accident is very painful and it will probably bleed. If it happens, apply pressure for up to five minutes until the bleeding stops. Alternatively, dip the toe into some wound powder made specifically for small animals; or put a blob of Vaseline, flour, or corn flour on the end of the wounded nail to seal it.

Baths

Ferrets do not need to be shampooed, unless on veterinary instructions or if they have got themselves into a mess that cannot be fixed by a gentle rub down or dip in lukewarm water. In fact, frequent bathing with shampoo is likely to increase that ferrety smell. This is because shampoo strips the fur of its essential oils and thus stimulates the skin to produce more. Giving your ferret the opportunity to play in fresh water will mostly suffice. If it is essential to use a shampoo, make sure you only use one that is suitable for small animals. Your vet will advise.

Bathe your ferret only if
it is really necessary.

Health
Conditions

Vaccinations

Ferrets can be vaccinated against two fatal diseases—distemper and rabies.

All ferrets, whether they are kept outdoors or not, should be vaccinated against distemper. It is a common, endemic disease in foxes and in some places in dogs, too. Ferrets should be first vaccinated when 12 weeks old and annually thereafter. If your adult ferret was not vaccinated when young, or has not been since, then get it done as soon as you can.

Keep him apart from other ferrets for at least two weeks. This quarantine period is to ensure he was not developing the disease before you had him vaccinated.

In the United States, it is recommended that all ferrets kept outdoors, or house ferrets taken out occasionally, are vaccinated against rabies.

Reasons for ferret vaccinations.

Opposite:
Flea control is important.

Illness and injuries

Accidents, injuries, or illness may happen and in the first instance a vet should be contacted to arrange treatment. But, in the time between the discovery of a problem and reaching the vet surgery you are responsible for providing the best care you can.

It is prudent to have a spare cage available if you have a sick or injured ferret.

Wounds

Bites from other ferrets are not common, except during mating, when the jill is likely to suffer wounds to her neck and shoulder. If injuries do occur at other times, this may indicate that your ferrets do not have enough space or things to do.

In the meantime, try to keep the wounded area as clean as possible. Prepare a solution of rock salt and warm water and cover the wound after washing to prevent any further risk of infection.

Most minor injuries can be treated at home with a salt wash solution and a cotton pad, but more serious injuries must be looked at and treated by a veterinarian as soon as possible to prevent infection and abscesses. If you have any doubt, take your ferret to the vet.

Injuries to the eyes can be more serious. You should contact your veterinarian at once if the eye is held closed or appears clouded. The sight in the eye, or the eye itself may be lost if treatment is delayed.

Constipation, diarrhea and sore stomachs

If you notice that your ferret has constipation or diarrhea you must contact a vet. These changes should be taken very seriously as they can have a number of causes, some of which, such as parvovirus, can be fatal. It may also mean that your ferret has eaten something poisonous, or more likely something that has caused an obstruction in his gut.

Obstructions can be caused by hairballs, fibers from towels or clothes, or bits of non-food items. A ferret with a sore stomach will pull its stomach in, so it seems flatter and sticks out at the sides, his back will be hunched and he will be restless and may scratch at the sides of his mouth. Surgery may be required, so do get veterinary advice as soon as possible.

Respiratory infections

Ferrets are prone to respiratory infections, including flu. Ferret symptoms are similar to our own: sneezing and coughing, runny nose and eyes. The ferret will be listless. If the discharge is clear then keep your ferret warm, with plenty of water and tempting food such as chicken and egg.

If the discharge from its nose is thick and pus-like, then seek veterinary advice. If in any doubt, consult your veterinarian.

Insulinoma

This is a form of diabetes where the blood sugar level drops due to excessive production of insulin. It is caused by tumors in the pancreas. Signs that your ferret may be suffering from this include a dribbling mouth, caused by excessive salivation, and general weakness. Your pet needs to see the vet.

Adrenal gland disease

A ferret that is losing weight, scratching a lot and getting bald spots, or drinking more than usual may have this disease, and needs veterinary attention.

Fits

Ferrets can suffer convulsions (fits) for a variety of reasons, including heatstroke or eating something poisonous. If you see your ferret having a fit, seek veterinary help right away.

Ears

Check to make sure your ferret's ears do not look sore or inflamed. The ear wax should be a yellow or reddish brown color. If it is black, then this may mean your ferret has ear mites, or some type of infection, and a trip to the vet is called for.

Fleas and ticks

Scratching and/or hair loss is a common symptom of skin complaints brought about by parasites such as fleas. Fleas can be a problem, as ferrets can be a host for the cat flea. Seek advice from your vet about an appropriate flea control.

Ticks can also be a problem, especially if your ferret has been used for hunting. They can be removed using a tick hook, obtainable from your vet.

Worms

Worms are rare in pet ferrets although tapeworms are potentially a problem. Symptoms include a distended abdomen and dry coat.

Obesity

Being overweight causes all sorts of problems for ferrets. It causes strain on the muscles and bones which can mean your ferret will be in pain. It can also lead to heart disease and make your ferret more prone to respiratory illness. It will both reduce the quality of your ferret's life and make that life shorter.

Ferret medicine

Veterinary knowledge of ferrets has increased hugely over the last few years and there is much more that can be done for your pet. However, unlike cat and dog medicine, which all veterinary surgeons know a lot about, ferrets are a specialist subject, and are actually considered an exotic species in terms of veterinary care. It is well worth finding a vet who is interested in ferrets and their treatment, and may even have a qualification in exotic animal medicine.

Know your pet ferret

Scientific name	Mustela putorius furo
Group order	Carnivora
Female breeding period	Induced ovulation
Gestation	42 days
Litter size	8 (average)
Birth weight	.25–.35 ounces (7-10 g)
Birth type	Naked, blind, dependent
Eyes open	28 days approx
Weaning	8 weeks
Breeding age	
Jill	9 months
Hob	9 months

Find Out More

Books

Morton, E. Lynn. *Ferrets* (Barron's Complete Pet Owner's Manual). New York: Barron's, 2000

Schilling, Kim. *Ferrets for Dummies*. New York: John Wiley/Dummies, 2007.

Web Sites

American Ferret Association, Inc
www.ferret.org

ASPCA
www.aspca.org

# Words to Understand

carcasses the dead bodies of animals

carnivores animals that eat meat

castration the removal of male reproductive organs

conformation the measurement of how much an animal matches the specific perfect traits for a particular breed

dimorphic when animals of the same breed differ greatly in appearance between genders

hob word for a male ferret

jill word for a female ferret

neutering the process of removing the reproductive organs of a female animal

microchipped given a tiny electronic implant that allows an animal to be tracked

physiological having to do with parts of a body

quick a noun meaning the part of the finger that holds a nail in place

Index